WORKING SAFELY

IN

CONFINED SPACES

By

Akanimo Etim Inwang

DEDICATION

This book is dedicated to all our frontline Personnel who are impacted, in one way or the other, while carrying out work activities in Confined Spaces.

APPRECIATION

My profound gratitude goes to my Mentor and Teacher Mr. E. L. Nwankwo who encouraged me to put these practical concepts in a book form for the continuous learning and growth of the Occupational Health and Safety Professionals.

I also appreciate my colleague Mr. Remigius Igweoji for assisting in various forms to ensuring the successful publishing of the book.

I appreciate my wife and children for the understanding, support and encouragement to making this book a reality.

I specially thank God Almighty for granting me the opportunity and empowerment to produce this book. May HIS Name alone be highly exalted forever, Amen.

FOREWORD

Working Safely in Confined Space is a book that discusses about Confined Spaces and Associated hazards, what to consider before entering a Confined Space, Confined Space Entry Emergency and rescue Response Procedure, Roles of Confined Space Entry work activity team members and Statutory Requirements for Safe Entry into Confined Space among others. The Author of this book, Akanimo Inwang, having gained much experience in Chemical processing plants and Oil and gas industry both from field and office deemed it fit to write this book to contribute his quota in saving lives from Confined Space related work activity.

I am recommending this book to all and sundry in all works of life, from Agricultural sector through Oil and gas to our individual homes. Let us join hands to eliminate death in confined Space work activity by implementing all the recommendations in this book.

Signed

Igweoji Remigius

TABLE OF CONTENTS

Page

INTRODUCTION

The advent of Industrial revolutions and technological advancement brought along with gains and increased productions, series of accidents and their corresponding adverse effects on humans, assets and environment, with many even losing their lives. These degenerated into serious "resources" crisis thus making responsible Governments to collaborate and issue guidelines that made Companies to streamline and coordinate their activities with a view to eliminating incidents occurrences due to work activities including confined Space entry as well as other identified potential factors (causes). In Nigeria, these guidelines are outlined in the FACTORIES' ACT (1990) and the WORKMEN COMPENSATION ACT (1990) and administered by the Federal Government of Nigeria and its assigned agencies.

Also, depending on the particular activities of the Organization, other Industry-related Regulations can apply. Such includes "The Confined Spaces Regulations 1997"; The Provision and use of Work Equipment Regulations 1998 (PUWER); Workplace (Health, Safety and Welfare) Regulations 1992; The Personal Protective Equipment Regulations 2002; and the Personal Protective Equipment at Work Regulations 1992 (as amended); The Mineral Oil (Safety) Regulations 1997 (which is under The Petroleum Act (CAP 350 LFN) of Nigeria, etc.

These guarantee the safety of Workers, Assets, Environment and, generally improve the Corporate Image of the Organization.

Safety in Industrial perspective refers to people's attitudes, habits, and activities in the provision and maintenance of an incident/accident-free safe working and living environment.
Safety is essential for sustainable human endeavors and more so in business settings where the statutes so mandate. Its contributions, occasionally though subtle, is essential for the key factors of business ventures like Human resources, Assets & Equipment, Environment, Finance and Corporate Image. The Corporate Image is derived from business sustainability which is in turn built on the collective maintenance of the integrity of these business factors.

Most Companies, based on their style, outlook and business nature, fashion their Vision, Mission Statement and HSE Policies ultimately with a view to creating a conducive business atmosphere for profitability and operating within regulatory statutes and, avoiding adverse or negative publicity. That is the basis of the often declared "Zero accident/incident Tolerance", which shows that, in every job or endeavor including Confined Space Entry, there is an accident factor or likelihood. This factor is undesired and decidedly unwanted. However, to ensure the achievement of this "ZERO TOLERANCE" to incidents occurrence, many Organizations have undertaken adequate trainings and enlightenment awareness campaigns for their workers to a level where all activities including Confined Space Entry can be performed without incident occurrence.

Accidents can be defined as an unexpected, unplanned event, in a sequence of events, that occurs through a combination of causes which can result in physical harm (injury/disease/death) to an individual or group of individuals; damage to property; a near-miss; a loss; or any combination of these effects.

The prevention of the manifestation of any of these said undesired factors is Safety at work. So, it is important to note that accidents are a people's problem which utilizes the unsafe acts and unsafe conditions created or established by man. When not checked or ineffectively controlled, the consequent event (accident) can lead to damage, injury or fatality. These **unsafe acts** and **unsafe conditions** that establish an accident potential are referred to as **Hazards**. Hence, hazards are agents (any object, situation, actions or behavior) which have the potential to cause harm (injury, ill health) or damage to property or the environment

Effect is the consequence of an unintended or undesired occurrence (accident). It is always an adverse effect on the Health or Safety of employees or the public.

The elimination of the different forms of hazard potentials, for the provision of safe work environment, is an important pre-occupation of organizations. To achieve this, a variety of measures are usually deployed. Some of these measures include; Engineering design, personnel training with follow-up reminders and, compliance monitoring with enforcement.

This catalogue of measures is what is usually referred to as HSE Management System (HSE-MS). It addresses the associated risks and proposes the means of their minimization and/or elimination. Some further assign responsibilities to achieve the goal.

The essence of implementation of the HSE-MS is the elimination of these hazard (risk) potentials at the task level of the organizations' activities. As stated earlier, but in more specific terms, these preventive measures can be grouped in the following forms;

- Engineering: Equipment type, design, layout, fit-for-purpose tools, etc.
- Administrative: Personnel training/refresher trainings, compliance monitoring/enforcement, etc.
- Statutory: Provision, and personnel use, of personal protective equipment (PPE), provision and maintenance of healthy and conducive work environment, basic welfare facilities, etc.

During design concepts for Plants installations, applicable engineering design of equipment and facilities and, layout, are carried out with the aim to economically maximizing the optimal and effective usage of available spaces for such installations. The consequence is that certain areas or parts of the premises may not be easily accessed anymore. These said restrictively accessed areas/spaces subsequently acquire secondary physical and environmental features that are likely to be detrimental to free and safe work and use by the personnel at any or certain times. Such spaces are referred to as CONFINED SPACES.

CONFINED SPACES can be described as anywhere there is inadequate natural ventilation. These may include such features as partial or complete enclosures with limited access that elevates the hazard potential.

From experience and observations, Confined space entry works are comparatively more difficult than similar works done in the open and free environment. This is because the working conditions in Confined Spaces are more hazardous. Such hazardous working conditions include, but not limited to: -

- Insecure footing
- Stagnant/foul air (which can lead to asphyxiation)
- Poor lighting/illumination
- Extremes of Temperature (excessive heat/cold)
- Lack of working space ("elbow-room")
- Noise (hearing)
- Etc.

Although the hazards involved in Confined spaces are well recognized and documented, accidents involving Confined

Space entry activities are still recorded annually. These serious and fatal injuries occur within a wide range of industries such as Chemical Plants complexes, Oil and Gas industries, Construction Industries, silos and storage tanks of Agricultural concerns, among others.

Those affected can include, not only those within the confined space(s) but also, the inexperienced who may ignorantly (or over-zealously) attempt rescue operations within the confined space. These may not have received adequate training for such emergency response.

Use of improper equipment (or equipment that are not fit-for-purpose) and, improper training of the personnel involved, can pre-dispose them and other rescue personnel to severe injuries.

To eliminate these types of incidents when work is done in confined space, it is good practice to develop (and ensure strict compliance to) safe "Confined Space Entry" Procedures. This procedure is developed with a view to providing maximum protection to all persons involved.

Most accidents occur because the people in charge: -
- Do not see or identify the hazards (what could occur)
- Under-estimate the risk involved
- Do not know what more that could be done to remove the hazards identified
- Allow standards of performance to slip

All these are human failings (errors).

This book is therefore intended for all who work in Industry especially those of Chemical, Oil & Gas and other Process Industries. It is also for those involved in Production, maintenance, design and construction activities at any level or in any capacity in carrying out work activities in Confined space(s).

It is also intended to act as a resource and guidance material to advise those responsible for such operations on the Safe Procedures and Precautions (or Safeguards) which are essential to achieving safe works in Confined Spaces.

CHAPTER ONE
CONFINED SPACES AND ASSOCIATED HAZARDS

CONFINED SPACE

Many work places contain spaces that are considered "CONFINED" because their configurations hinder the activities of employees who must enter, work in or pass through them.

Confinement here refers to spaces that are relatively small and restricted/limited air volume, unfavorable natural ventilation and, where dangerous air contamination cannot be prevented or quickly removed by natural means through existing opening(s) within the enclosure.

Confined space accidents are of particular concern in occupational health and safety due to the hazards that they pose to the victim and subsequently to a rescue team. Also, some places may become confined spaces when work is being carried out, or during their construction, fabrication or subsequent modification.

A Confined space can be described as any space that has limited or restricted means for entry or exit, inadequate natural ventilation and, is not designed for continuous personnel occupancy.

It is described as an area whose enclosed condition and limited access make it dangerous.

Confined space can also be described as a place which is substantially enclosed (though not always entirely), and

where serious injury can occur from hazardous substances or conditions within the space or nearby. These hazardous substances often include harmful dust or gases, asphyxiants, submersion in liquids or free-flowing granular solids (for example, grain bins), electrocution, or entrapment.

Because of the additional special hazards presented by Confined Spaces, entry into such Confined Spaces require special and documented permissions by responsible persons or authorities.

Such permit-requiring Confined Spaces entry activities include those that: -

- Contain or have the potential to contain a hazardous atmosphere
- Contain material(s) that has the potential to engulf an entrant
- Have restricted natural ventilation or contain material(s) that has the potential to deplete the Oxygen concentration within the confined space to less than 19.5%
- Have walls that converge inward or, floors that slope downward and taper into a smaller area which could trap an entrant
- Contain any other recognized safety or health hazard such as unguarded machinery, exposed live-wires, etc.

Confined Spaces can thus be found in virtually anywhere and therefore be encountered in any occupation (even at homes). They come in different shapes, sizes and, can also be located above or below the ground.

The following, and their likes, would also constitute Confined Spaces: - Tanks; storage bins; process vessels; silos; pits; underground utility vaults; pipeline; wells; culverts; hoppers; sewers; tank-cars; rail-cars; aircraft wings; ship-holds; poorly ventilated rooms; tunnels; ditches/trenches; etc.

Note that certain Trenches also qualify as Confined spaces due to a variety of features like limited access/egress.

It is also of importance to note that a space that was presumed to be safe and "un-confined" can easily become a Confined Space due to prevailing circumstances and, in many cases, the occupants are usually unaware of this new "confined space" status:

Example 1: A trench which is deep enough to make the occupant's head to be seen below the ground surface (about 50cm below grade) and, located within the surroundings of a process plant where heavier-than-air gases leak (or with fugitive emissions), and; depending on wind direction, these gases may flow into such trench and displace enough air for the Oxygen levels to decrease to less than 19.5%.

Example 2: Depending on the prevailing wind direction, the practice of stationing "operating" electric power generating sets near living rooms (perhaps for security purposes) that have only single windows (that is, not two windows located on opposite sides for cross ventilation) predisposes the occupancy to inadvertent Carbon-monoxide poisoning.

In the two examples above, prevailing wind-bearing gaseous emissions displace enough Oxygen concentration in the "spaces" to qualify them as hazardous confined spaces. It is also to be noted that if the gases displacing the Oxygen concentrations in the "spaces" are odorless (like the Carbon monoxide in example 2), the occupant(s) may not be aware of the presence of these gases and the consequent hazard they are being exposed to.

In summary, Confined Space is a fully or partially enclosed space that:

- is not primarily designed or intended for continuous human occupancy
- has limited or restricted entrance or exit, or a configuration that can complicate first aid, rescue, evacuation, or other emergency response activities
- Can represent a risk for the health and safety of anyone who enters, due to one or more of the following factors:
    - its design, construction, location or atmosphere
    - the materials or substances in it
    - work activities carried out previously or, being carried out in it,
    - mechanical, process and safety hazards present

Pictures of examples of Confined Spaces

Figure 1 Storage Tank

Figure 2 Process Vessels

Figure 3: Man-hole

Figure 4: Confined Space Entry in progress

ASSOCIATED HAZARDS IN CONFINED SPACES

Serious accidents have occurred and continue to occur while work is being done within Confined Spaces. The chief risks are those associated with the following: -

- Toxic and/or flammable gases
- Fumes and vapors

- Sudden uncontrolled release of energy such as mechanical, electrical, high pressure fluids, etc.
- Neglect or ignorance of the necessary precautions

Any of these can lead, very easily, to accidents; a significant number of which are (and can be) fatal. Multiple fatalities are not uncommon.

Most hazards found in regular worksites can also be found in confined spaces. However, they can be more hazardous in confined spaces than in a regular worksite. This is because of the peculiar characteristic configuration of Confined Spaces.

These hazards include the following:
A. **OXYGEN DEFICIENCY**: There may be an insufficient concentration of Oxygen in the air for the worker to breathe.

This condition can be due the following: -

1. A process of purging the Confined space with an inert gas (e.g. Nitrogen gas) to remove flammable or toxic gas or vapor

2. Formation of oxidation products on the inner surface of the Confined space, such as a vessel/tank constructed particularly of steel material which had been left completely closed for some time, where the Oxygen in the air in the Confined space is used up by the oxidation process on the inner surface(s) of the Confined Space.

3. Oxygen deficiency in drains, pits, etc., may be caused by ingress of Methane gas or utilization of

Oxygen by certain microbes or other constituents of the soil.

B. **TOXIC GASES**: The atmosphere may contain a poisonous/toxic gas (or substance) that can make the worker ill or even lose consciousness. This can result from dangerous concentrations of such gases/vapors arising from sources both within and outside the Confined space. Possible examples include: -

1. Gas/vapor remaining from a process/activity which has previously been carried on in the Confined space.
2. Gas/vapor which enters the Confined space from adjourning plant through piping inlets from which it has not been effectively isolated
3. Fumes emitted when sludge or other deposits in the Confined space are disturbed during cleaning or other activities
4. Fumes produced by the task being performed inside the Confined space. Such tasks include but not limited to welding; flame-cutting; hand brushing or power brushing and spray painting; use of adhesives or solvents; etc.
5. The product of combustion of various fuels, e.g. carbon monoxide from a fuel-powered internal combustion engine inside the Confined space or nearby
6. Oxygen enrichment of the atmosphere caused by operations which involve an excess of Oxygen e.g. Oxy-propane cutting. This also present the risk of

enhanced combustibility and possible spontaneous combustion/explosion

C. **UN-CONTROLLED RELEASE OF ENERGY:** This includes: -
   1. Electrical energy which can cause electric shocks, electrocution, burns, fire, etc.
   2. Mechanical energy in such Confined spaces that have un-guarded and exposed rotating machinery such as Agitators/Stirrers. If these machineries are started accidentally, this can lead to injury or even death of the occupant(s)
   3. High pressure fluids, which can be Process-related such as steam, residual chemicals, etc. This can lead to the exposure of persons working inside the Confined space to chemicals through skin contact, ingestion or inhalation of the contaminated air. This can cause suffocation, unconsciousness, burns (from temperature extremes of the incoming fluids), drowning, etc.

D. **FIRE HAZARD:** There may be an explosive/flammable atmosphere in the Confined space due to the presence of flammable liquids/gas (with concentrations within their flammability ranges) and combustible dusts which if ignited can lead to fire or explosion.

E. **SHIFTING OR COLLAPSING BULK MATERIALS:** Free-flowing solid materials, such as grains, can partially solidify in silos (or powdered raw materials in storage bins) causing blockages which can collapse unexpectedly

F. **MECHANICAL HAZARDS** such as presented by moving parts of associated equipment (e.g. unguarded mechanical stirrers or agitators). Others include entanglement, crushing, slips, trips, falls, etc.

G. **BARRIER FAILURE** which can result in a flood or release of free-flowing solid materials. Also, in Civil Construction industry, collapse of trench walls on to workers within the trench can cause injuries and/or even fatalities. This is usually the reason for the shoring of the walls of such trenches. If not properly done, the shoring can also fail with consequent adverse effects.

H. **BIOLOGICAL HAZARDS** such as entering an abandoned confined space which is now inhabited by dangerous reptiles, etc.

I. **TEMPERATURE EXTREMES** with hot conditions leading to a dangerous increase in body temperature as well as cold conditions (e.g. prolonged stay in cold-room can lead to unpleasant freezing effects).

J. **OTHER NON-MECHANICAL HAZARDS** including poor visibility, poor illumination; noise; radiation; vibration; etc.

K. **ACCESS AND EGRESS:** if access into the Confined space is through a restricted entrance such as a man-hole, escape or rescue in an emergency situation will be more difficult

All tasks/activities have their inherent hazards and, it is important to note that not all the hazards can lead to accident occurrence. What leads to accident occurrence is how the inherent hazards are controlled.

Having identified the possible hazards to be encountered in a Confined space, it is important to plan to control them with a view to ensuring that the task is performed safely. This is in line with the Safety Principle which states that "ALL ACCIDENTS ARE PREVENTABLE".

The next Chapter will highlight the control methods for handling the various inherent hazards encountered in Confined Space entry activities.

CHAPTER TWO

PREPARATION FOR CONFINED SPACE ENTRY

In considering entry into Confined Space for any activity, it is worthy to note that all Confined Spaces such as tanks (whether big, small, located underground or above the ground) are dangerous. Hence, regardless of size, shape, position or other characteristics, **all Confined Spaces should be considered Hazardous.**

Before venturing into confined space entry, the following have to be considered

1. **Inherent Hazards'**

A conscious and careful study of the activity to be carried out needs to be done in order to identify and assess the inherent hazards to be encountered in the operation; check and put in place, control measures to counter the identified and assessed hazards. Also, adequate recovery measures to mitigate the adverse effects that may occur in situations where the control measures are not completely effective enough to prevent accident.

This is generally referred to as Hazard and Effects Management System (HEMP). A typical example of this is the Job Safety Analysis (JSA) which identify the inherent hazards in the activity, how such hazards can be controlled to avoid accident occurrence and, Recovery measures including Emergency Response Procedures.

2. Access and Egress

This can be the opening through which one can enter the Confined space and also, come out of the Confined space. Questions like the following can be asked: "is the size of the opening big enough to allow workers wearing all the necessary equipment to climb in and out easily and provide ready access and egress in an emergency?"

The size of the opening may require choosing air-line breathing apparatus in place of a Self-Contained Breathing Apparatus (SBCA) which is bulkier and therefore likely to restrict ready passage. SBCA as such is better used in spaces that have unrestricted access/egress.

The shape and size of the opening should be assessed whether it meets statutory requirements with the objective of knowing whether it will hinder access or "quick" egress. The edge of the opening should also be assessed with a view to ascertaining whether it is sharp or smooth or rough. This will give a clear picture on precautions to be taken while entering and exiting the Confined space; equipment and/or accessories like cables and hoses that could be passed into Confined space (as the sharp edges can damage the cables and hoses if not properly protected); rescue procedures; etc.

3. Removal of Materials from the Confined Space

All materials, whether solid, liquid or gas, which are liable to present a hazard to person(s) inside the Confined space should be removed completely.

It should be borne in mind that these materials can give rise to hazardous atmosphere (in the Confined space) causing effects such as asphyxiation; or the worker(s) may be drowned in liquid or covered in solid materials (such as grains, sand, etc.)

Also, in considering the possibility of dangerous gas or vapor being present, account should be taken of the previous uses of the Confined space as well as its immediate use prior to entry.

The previous use can predispose the Confined space to the presence of incident-causative factors such as: -

- Solvent-laden sludge or residues
- Vaporization of toxic residues/fumes by hot works
- Displacement of caked toxic materials
- Possible reactions between residues and the materials being used while performing the tasks
- Etc.

Hence, some Confined spaces need to be scrupulously cleaned before any entry is made.

The evacuation of the materials from, and the cleaning of, the Confined space can be done through drain valves, opened man-way/man-hole (as applicable) using appropriate and notable safe methods.

The method to be used in cleaning the Confined space has to be assessed for inherent hazards and precautions taken into consideration. Such methods may include: -

- Steam cleaning
- Partial filling with water, boiling it and then, drained

- Washing with hot (and/or cold water)
- Use of solvents and neutralizing agents. This needs extreme caution as they generate combustible atmosphere or involve exothermic reactions
- Purging

Purging is a process where liquids/vapors remaining in the Confined space are removed by natural or induced draft. Atmospheric air or inert gas can be used for the purging process.

Inert gas (usually nitrogen gas) are mainly used to purge plants / Confined spaces with suspected presence of flammable gas or vapor to avoid the formation of explosive mixture with air.

However, inert gases do not support life hence, if entry into the Confined space that has been purged with inert gas is to be made without the use of breathing apparatus, atmospheric air has to be used to also purge off the inert gas from the Confined space.

The Confined space will thereafter be properly tested, before entry is made, to confirm that the oxygen concentration is within acceptable limits for life sustenance (without presenting asphyxiation and, fire hazards).

4. Isolation

If gas, fume or vapor can enter the Confined space into which entry for work activity is to be made, appropriate physical isolation of all the associated pipe-work has to be carried out. Also, mechanical and electrical isolation of associated equipment are essential if the equipment can otherwise operate, or be operated inadvertently.

Note that under certain conditions, a proper electrical isolation goes beyond de-energization from the breaker and tagging at the motor control centers (MCC), but has to include actual disconnection of the supply line.

However, in all cases, a check should be made to ensure isolation is effective.

The majority of Tanks and Vessels (and other Confined spaces) have one or more openings through which flow various liquid or gaseous raw materials, in-process materials, or finished products through pipeline connections; as well as other types of openings. These materials may be water, solvents, oil, acids, inert gas, steam, combustible/flammable gas, etc.

Ingress of any of such materials in the "occupied" Confined spaces while work is going on, through any of these openings which might have been isolated through isolation elements such as closed but leaking valve, etc., can lead to serious and sometimes fatal accidents. Therefore, **all pipelines, ducts and, other associated openings should be blanked and/or disconnected as applicable before anyone enters the Confined space.**

In process plant, when a whole unit is shut down for an extended maintenance, the usual practice is to isolate the unit at the "Battery Limit" by inserting Blank flanges in all relevant pipelines to obstruct fluid(s) from entering the unit and ultimately, the Confined space.

The individual Confined spaces that are to be entered are then isolated by blanking or disconnection and not solely dependent on valve isolation alone as valves can leak (in most cases, un-noticed).

The point at which the disconnection or blanking is made has to be recorded and tagged so that the line cannot be put to service while work is still going on in the Confined space.

Some Confined spaces (like reaction Drums/Tanks) have mechanical devices for various purposes. These devices include Agitators/stirrers, etc. Some are attached to a set of gear systems which make the entire reaction Drum to rotate while in normal operation. If they are accidentally started while work is going on inside the Confined space, it can lead to fatal accidents. Therefore, all powered equipment or devices inside or associated with the Confined space should be appropriately de-energized, disconnected, locked out and tagged out (LOTO) at the point of the power source, before any person enters the Confined space.

An example of a point of electrical power source is a circuit breaker of the power device located in the motor control center (MCC) of the Plant. It is therefore of much importance that the LOCKOUT and TAG-OUT (LOTO) Procedure be strictly adhered to before entry into Confined space that is equipped with powered device(s) is made.

5. Ventilation

All safe Confined space entry procedures include protection against the Hazard of suffocation.

Although they may vary depending upon the type of Confined space and other details, all specific protections against suffocation have one important feature in common; they all ensure that the man in the Confined space has a supply of uncontaminated air for breathing.

Ventilation of a Confined space is to remove contaminated air from the Confined space and replace it with air suitable for breathing.

This can be achieved through natural air drafts or through mechanical devices to generate forced air drafts across the Confined space via the available openings in the Confined space.

The mechanical devices may include the use of: -

- Electrically powered Blower to ventilate the Confined space
- Venturi-type Air Mover to suck out the air in the Confined space thereby forcing fresh air from the outside into the Confined space through other available opening(s)

Figure 5: Example of Forced Ventilation setup

Figure 5 shows an example of forced ventilation setup using blower as a mechanical air moving device

In some cases, continuous ventilation may not eliminate air contamination from the Confined space. In such a situation, a decision has to be made on how best to ensure that the personnel entering the Confined space has adequate uncontaminated air to breathe.

Provision of suitable Breathing Apparatus to the person entering the Confined space is essential if the space cannot be made fit to breathe because of the presence of gas, fume or vapor. A hose-mask linked to a remotely located (outside the Confined space) air blower or, an air-line mask supplied by air cylinders or flow-regulated air from air compressor can be used to ensure availability of adequate breathing air for the person inside the Confined space.

The person entering the Confined space where breathing air is to be supplied remotely should be provided with an additional portable and functional air cylinder that can be linked to the airline mask in emergency situations where the remote air source fails. This type of breathing apparatus is usually referred as Dual-purpose Self-Contained Breathing Apparatus (SCBA).

It is to be noted that it is not advisable to enter a Confined space with Self Contained Breathing Apparatus (SCBA) through man-hole as this can hinder rescue operations.
It is also advisable never to try to "sweeten" the air in a Confined space with oxygen as this can greatly increase the risk of a fire or explosion.

6. Atmospheric Gas Testing

We all know that impure or contaminated air often neither smells, looks, nor tastes much different than fresh air. Typical examples include: -

- The deadly carbon monoxide (CO), an asphyxiation hazard which can be obtained from carbon-fuel internal combustion engines' exhaust
- Natural gas which is a serious fire hazard; etc.

Hence, a Confined space atmospheric Gas testing is necessary to check that it is free from both toxic and flammable gases/vapors as well as fit for breathing.

Figure 6: Gas Testing

Gas-testing should be carried out by a competent person using a suitable and fit-for-purpose Gas Detector (Gas Tester, Explosimeter, etc.) which is correctly calibrated.

Where the Risk Assessment indicates that conditions in the Confined space may change, or as a further precaution, continuous monitoring of the air in the Confined space may be necessary.

As far as possible, tests should be made from outside the Confined space, drawing in the air sample through suitable sample probes before entering into the Confined space.

Care should be taken to ensure that air is tested throughout the Confined space; side-to-side and, top-to-bottom. **Obtaining samples from isolated/peculiar areas or edges of the Confined space can be very dangerous as it may not give a true picture of the air content of the Confined space.** Any sludge present should be disturbed to release any trapped gases or vapor before testing.

The test should show that: -

- The oxygen content is within acceptable (safe) limits; that is, not too little (oxygen-deficient) and not too much (fire-hazard) in the range of 19.5% - 21%
- A hazardous atmosphere (toxic gases, flammable atmosphere) is not present
- Ventilation equipment is operating properly (where such is required)

The results of the tests and time have to be properly documented. Where traces of sludge remain, a re-test 30-45 minutes (depending on the Risk Assessment recommendations) after the initial test may be essential prior to entry.

7. Illumination

It is required that the illumination inside a Confined space in which work is to be carried out be made to be as bright as daylight illumination.

Therefore, where the entry requires illumination, a good source should be provided, preferably **approved explosion-proof type**. It should be powered by an approved and, acceptable low voltage source (usually of maximum voltage not exceeding 25-36 volts). Residual Current Devices (RCDs) can also be used.

This low voltage is essential to prevent electrocution in event of the power cord burning up or being broken and makes contact with the vessel, the low voltage will not cause serious injury (or electrocution) if contacted by or conducted (as in cases involving metallic tanks) to the person(s) working in the Confined Space.

Depending on the nature and location of the Confined Space, it is advisable to carry along a standby battery-powered portable light source, such as a flash light, while making entry in case the natural or artificial illumination source fails.

8. Personal Protective Equipment

Personal protective equipment (PPE) are pieces of equipment and apparels used or worn by a worker to protect him/her against the hazards inherent in his/her work activity (after all other control measures have been put in place to mitigate such and other hazards).

They (PPE) minimize the effect of the inherent (residual) hazards on the worker and/or, mitigate the severity of the adverse effect emanating from an accident occurrence on the worker.

Figure 7: Confined Space Entry Team

Therefore, Confined Space entry requires the wearing of protective equipment to safeguard all parts of the body that may be exposed to possible injury.

Some of the basic PPE that may be required include: -

- Hard hat for head protection
- Coverall/work clothes for body protection
- Gloves for hands and fingers protection (which can be task-specific)
- Safety shoes for feet and toes protection
- Safety glasses for eye protection

The use of other PPE may be dependent on the nature of the task to be performed and also, the outcome of the Risk Assessment with regards to the task and, emergency rescue, if such need arises.

These may include: -

- Hearing protection (ear plugs/ear muffs)
- Welders' suits, gloves, masks, etc.

- Safety harnesses and lanyards (and/or lifeline)

9. OTHER CONSIDERATIONS

Other considerations occasionally relevant for Confined Space entry work may include: -

A. Non-sparking Tools: Provision of non-sparking tools (e.g. Brass hammer, etc.) for use in potentially explosive atmospheres.

B. Means of access/egress: Provision of ladder where necessary. This should be fastened to a fixed structure.

C. Earthing/Bonding: Where there is a danger of static electric discharge which can cause a fire or explosion, special precautions e.g. earthing and bonding have to be done.

D. Rest Periods: Based on the nature of the work and the Risk Assessment, the work duration should be periodically interrupted. If the activity is carried out underground or within trenches, the worker can exit the Confined space and rest at intervals in the open before re-commencement of his/her task or, the task could be rostered among the workers for staggered short interval work durations

E. Communication: The mode and means of Communication between the entrant and attendant need to be agreed upon before entry into the Confined space. Communication Gadgets such as: - 2-way Radio communication sets; Cameras; Close-Circuit Television

(CCTV) system, and the use of lanyard may be provided depending on the task requirements.

F. Method of transferring materials: The method of transferring materials into, and out of the Confined space also need to be considered after assessing the type, shape and weight of the materials involved. *It is to be noted that materials should not be thrown into and out of an "occupied" Confined space.* Also, entrant should not hand carry any material when going in or out of confined space.

G. Attendant: Personnel inside a Confined space should be kept under constant observation by the standby person, the "Attendant or watchman", positioned outside the Confined space (or continuously monitored on the relevant console using CCTV system as applicable). Where a lifeline or lanyard is in use, care should be taken to ensure that it does not become entangled on pipes and fittings.

H. Training: All persons to be involved in Confined space entry activity need to be properly trained with a view to creating awareness on the inherent hazards involved, and the precautions to be taken while carrying out activities in Confined space(s). These persons include: -
- Supervisors
- Persons likely to enter the Confined spaces to carry out work in them
- Persons likely to act as Standby personnel (Watcher)
- Persons appointed to form an Emergency Rescue Team.

Instruction in the use of equipment can often usefully be done by the manufacturer or, by using the manufacturer's instruction manual. Hence, it is important to keep and make available as required, the manufacturer's Instruction and maintenance Manual.

The training should be re-enforced by Rescue scenario practices such as Emergency Response Drills and, Refresher Courses, Job Safety Analysis (JSA) or Job Hazard Analysis (JHA), Tool-Box Talks (prior to the Confined space entry), etc.

In addition to the trainings for the personnel likely to be involved in the Confined space entry activity, there is a related need to ensure that person(s) who are likely to carry out the atmospheric air tests are properly trained and made competent in the use of the air test equipment provided. Such training should include: -

- A basic understanding of the mode of operation of the equipment;
- The method(s) of use of the equipment;
- The limitation(s) of the equipment;
- The interpretations of the result(s);
- Maintenance and calibration of the equipment as applicable.

I. **Personnel Fitness Assurance:** All the personnel for the Confined Space entry activities should be medically and physically certified fit for the activities by approved relevant professional(s)/institution(s).

CHAPTER THREE

CONFINED SPACE ENTRY EMERGENCY AND RESCUE RESPONSE PROCEDURE

Entering a **confined-space** can be deadly. All personnel for Confined Space Entry must have a complete understanding of what to do in the event of a confined-space emergency and ways to avoid such an incident. When things go wrong, people may be exposed to serious and immediate danger. Effective arrangements for raising alarm and carrying out rescue operations in an emergency are essential. The importance of the standby personnel (attendant) positioned outside the Confined space (or the CCTV console) can never be over-emphasized in this regard.

Contingency Plans will depend on the nature of the Confined space, the potential hazard scenario and the work to be carried out. These determine the rescue nature including the applicable rescue equipment such as: -

- *Ambulance with First-Aid and resuscitation kits*
- *Man-Baskets*
- *Arm and leg splint*
- *Tripod and winch*
- *Etc., depending on the outcome of the Risk Assessment*

Considerations for effective Emergency Response include the following:

* All the personnel involved in the Emergency response need to be properly trained to carry out their functions effectively; to be always alert and available and; be capable of using any equipment provided for the rescue operations.
* Attendant should know the emergency contact numbers
* Attendant and other emergency rescue team should not leave the scene except that the release of hazard could also affect them.
* Rescuers should not go into confined space for their rescue operations
* Rescuers also need to be protected against the cause of the emergency.
* Trained First-Aider(s) should be available to make proper use of any necessary First-Aid equipment provided;
* Consideration should be made concerning, where applicable, the need to shut down adjacent Plant(s)/Unit(s) before attempting emergency rescue;
* Local and other Emergency services available can also be of use in events of escalated situations. Consideration of aligning the Organization's Emergency Response Procedure with external Emergency Response Services may not be out of place. This may be of assistance in serious case(s), hence, the mode of communication with them in such cases need to be considered in the Emergency Response Plan.

CHAPTER FOUR
DECISION FOR CONFINED SPACE ENTRY

Once the Risk Assessment is completed, a decision has to be made, based on the assessment, on whether Confined Space Entry should be done; **or**, the work can be done in an alternative way such that entry into the Confined space is avoided.

However, such alternative ways that may eliminate Confined space entry activity may include: -

- Modifying the Confined space itself so that entry is not necessary
- Having the work done from outside the Confined space, e.g.
    - ❖ Blockages can be cleared in silos by use of remotely operated rotating flail devices, vibrators. Air-purgers, etc.
    - ❖ Inspection, sampling and, cleaning operations can be done from outside the Confined space using appropriate equipment and tools
    - ❖ Remote Cameras can be used for internal inspection of vessels

However, if entry into the Confined space cannot be avoided, a safe system for working inside the Confined space has to be developed and put to practice. This will be based on the result of the Risk Assessment made. This will help in identifying the necessary precaution(s) to reduce the risk of injury.

Every personnel involved will need to be properly trained and adequately informed/instructed to be sure he/she knows what to do and how to do it safely, thereby complying with the provisions of the Safe System of Work (SSW) developed and put to practice.

The next Chapter will handle the development and use of Safe Systems of Work (SSW) for accomplishing tasks inside the Confined space safely.

CHAPTER FIVE

CONFINED SPACE ENTRY

Relevant Confined Space Entry Safety Principles:
- *All accidents are preventable*
- *All injuries are preventable*
- *Each employee has the responsibility to work safely*
- *Ask yourself; "What must I do to keep myself from being hurt, and keep from hurting others?"*

- *Always;*
    - *Obtain Supervisory Authorization before entering tanks or other Confined spaces*
    - *Follow approved Confined space entry Procedures*
    - *Use approved Confined space entry equipment*

- *PLANNING FOR SAFETY*
    - *GET READY:*
        - *Get the big picture*
        - *Prepare for the unexpected*
        - *Let others know what you are doing*
    - *DO:*
        - *Follow Safety Rules and Procedures*
        - *Be alert for changing or unusual conditions*
    - *PUT AWAY:*
        - *Leave job in safe condition*

Confined space Entry (CSE) should only be considered when no alternative method is available. Once it has been decided that entry into the Confined space cannot be avoided, a safe system for working inside the Confined space has to be developed based on the task to be performed inside the Confined space and the consequent Risk Assessment.

This Risk Assessment should involve consideration of: -

- The work required to be done
- The method(s) by which the task can be performed
- The inherent hazards in the Plant in relation to the task and the method proposed

For Confined space entry to be achieved safely, the following conditions have to be satisfied: -

- Development of a safe system of work
- Obtaining a duly endorsed Confined space entry authorizations with stipulations of the work-related precautions including applicable atmospheric air tests, mode of communication specified, Lockout/Tag-out (LOTO), isolations/disconnections done and, tools/equipment for the job specified, certified and approved for use
- Consideration of the prevailing atmospheric temperature in the Confined space and making sure that it is adequate for entry
- Means for entry and egress and, Emergency Response procedures specified

- Compliance to the specified conditions for safe work communicated to work crew (for strict compliance)

After being satisfied that the above conditions are met, the Confined space entry work can commence.

However, while performing the task within the Confined space, try not to yield to pressure and complacency to go against the provisions in the various safe systems of work developed and put to practice concerning the task being performed.

SAFE SYSTEM OF WORK

Due to the various inherent hazards and subsequent Risk involved in Confined Space entry work activities, it is important that Organizations have written procedure or instructions for the activity.

In this context, Safe System of work refers to the various deliberate approaches by the Organization in line with statutory requirements and good practices to achieving its confined space entry work activities safely; hence, management commitment to its development and putting to practice, with adequate training of the workforce for effective compliance to it, is very important for achieving SAFE WORK.

Safe Work Method Statement (WMS) and Practice: This can generally be referred to as a set of written methods outlining how to perform a Confined Space entry task with minimum risk to the people, equipment, materials, environment and processes. It is developed based on the outcome of the Risk Assessment carried out on a particular confined space activity to be performed and broadcast to the workforce. It is usually achieved by making copies accessible to the workers and training them as required and, highlighting same at Tool-Box meetings.

Safe Work Procedure: This document specifies the method and tools to be used in performing the confined space task and, the competency of those to perform the task. In some cases, it includes the safe work method statements and Job safety analysis (JSA) or Job hazard analysis (JHA).

Job Safety Analysis (JSA): It is a series of specific steps that guide a work through a particular confined space task from start to finish in a sequential order designed to reduce the risk involved by minimizing potential exposure. It is usually developed by experienced competent personnel who might be from different inter-related disciplines and work crew representative(s) and, cascaded to the workers as part of training.
It is a written document prepared to highlight the following:
-

- The inherent hazards identified in the task to be performed
- The precautions to be taken to prevent incident occurrence, Recovery measures such as Emergency response plans put in place to rescue life in case things go wrong while the task is being performed, etc.

CONDITIONS OF EQUIPMENT

For enhanced potential hazards' elimination prior to Confined space entry, added to the Job Safety Analysis (JSA) and Tool-Box meeting, few selected experienced craftsmen ought to re-check thoroughly all the equipment, tools and PPE to be used for the assignment; all defective ones promptly taken out of service and, replaced by fit-for-purpose ones. They shall also confirm that all relevant Emergency Response equipment are fit-for-purpose and available for use at any time.

Basic relevant emergency and rescue procedures are also, essential issues to be highlighted and understood during the pre-entry Tool-Box meeting.

PERMIT-TO-WORK (PTW)

This is a document that identifies precisely: -

- The location of confined space entry activity
- The prevalent hazards
- the necessary precautions to be put in place to perform the task safely.
- The authorization for the work to commence and, when the validation will expire.

It is to be noted that if a job is not defined precisely, errors are likely to be made which can lead to injuries/harm

As indicated by (HSE-1980) "working safely in Confined spaces where there is likelihood of danger from gas or vapor or, where there is likely to be a deficiency of oxygen for breathing purposes, depends entirely on strict adherence to a well-devised system of precautions. As it is essential that such precautions are followed without exception on every occasion, the system is best laid down in writing in the form of a 'Permit-to-work' system.

A Permit-to-work (PTW) is essentially a document which sets out the work to be done and the precautions to be taken while carrying out the task

It pre-determines a safe work procedure where all foreseeable hazards have been considered in advance and that all appropriate precautions are defined and taken in correct sequence."

It does not in itself make the job safe; it is dependent on the effectiveness of the persons concerned adhering strictly to the provisions of the PTW.

The PTW in relation to Confined space entry is usually referred to as CONDINED SPACE ENTRY PERMIT.

Confined Space Entry Permit: This is a special written Permit, properly filled out and signed by designated Responsible person(s). It can also be referred to as "Supervisory Authorization" for entry into Confined space.

This Permit varies depending on the type of work, equipment and hazards that may be encountered.

In some Organizations, the Confined Space Entry Permit is issued as a complimentary Permit to the main work activity permit issued for the work activities to be carried out in the Confined space at that time.

The following are some of the reasons for using Confined space entry permits: -

- To help ensure that all possible safety precautions are taken for the protection of persons entering the Confined space
- To provide an orderly, systemic check of all safety items to ascertain their conditions
- To establish that the responsible supervisory personnel have authorized the Confined space entry and the work involved
- To provide a written record of the Confined space entry and;
- Generally, to state guidelines for achieving the work goal while preserving facilities and resources

Extra care should be taken to re-enforce the understanding and strict compliance to all the Permit stipulations by all personnel involved.

Management therefore should demonstrate a consistent support to enforcing a strict compliance to those relevant safety measures geared towards health, life, materials, facilities and environmental resource preservation and sustainable utilization

It should be noted, in this respect, that management has a duty in law to ensure a safe place of work and means of access to/egress from that place of work for every person working in the Organization's facility including Contractor(s)' employees. Care should be taken to satisfy this responsibility, among others.

TASK REVIEW BEFORE ENTRY INTO CONFINED SPACE

Prior to entry into the Confined space, it is vital that the task to be performed be reviewed in detail with the Supervisor before starting the job so as to avoid any misunderstanding which could be critical if delayed until work is already underway in the Confined space.

Also, all members of the work crew should review the Procedure for a harmonized understanding of the relevant work and potential Emergency Response Procedures. This review is done with the entire work crew during the mandatory Tool-Box meeting prior to entry into the Confined space.

CHAPTER SIX
CONFINED SPACE ENTRY TEAM

Because of the great number of potential hazards inherent in Confined spaces, works within any Confined space is never a simple matter. Cooperative efforts of all persons involved are needed to ensure the safety of personnel involved.

In essence, Confined space work is a good example of a situation where coordinated team effort is of utmost importance.

In selecting the Confined space Entry Team, depending on the nature of task(s) to be performed inside the Confined space, the following categories of persons, depending on their functions, may be selected into the team: -

1. The person(s) that will perform the task in the Confined space
2. The standby Watch-man(attendant) at the Confined space opening
3. The Confined space atmospheric air tester who makes the oxygen and flammable vapor/gas tests
4. The person that will operate the Air-blower or, be in charge of the breathing air supply Console Unit (and/or the person that shall be in charge of the CCTV console)
5. The person that will perform the isolation Lock-out and Tag-out procedure
6. The person that will hold the lifeline.

They have to be adequately trained and made to comprehensively understand the applicable Confined space entry Procedure to be able to handle his/her assigned responsibility efficiently as any error or negligence in their activity/action/responsibility can lead to accident, injury or even fatality.

FUNCTIONS OF CONFINED SPACE ENTRY TEAM

1. **Host Employer (property owner/manager):** Provides information on known "permit space(s)" and hazards/potential hazards and precautions used to protect employees in the space(s) to the controlling contractor

2. **Competent Person:**
   - Identifies all confined spaces and those which require a permit

   - Evaluates each space (testing if necessary)

   - Post signs or otherwise inform employees of the dangers

   - Informs the controlling contractor and the employees' authorized representative.

   - Reevaluates a non-permit space if there are any changes that might increase the hazards

   - Reclassifies a permit space as a non-permit space, only if:
     - There are no hazards present

     - The hazards have been eliminated or isolated (forced air ventilation is not elimination or isolation)

- o Certification exists in writing of the elimination/isolation of all hazards
- o Reclassify a non-permit space if any hazards arise and evacuate all employees from the space

3. Entry Supervisors:

- He/she is a Qualified person assigned by employers to determine if acceptable entry conditions are present in a permit space, to authorize entry, oversee operations and terminate them as required.
- The Supervisor has to be a person that is well experienced practically and technically on the type of task to be performed; the Confined space and the Plant activities.
- Based on his experience, he shall select competent persons for the job. While selecting the competent persons for the job, the following factors shall be considered: -
    - o Their physical built in relation to the layout of the Confined space
    - o Their psychological state (e.g. fear)
    - o Their medical condition as advised by the Medical Doctor

Therefore, in pursuance of the achievement of safe works, Supervisors should be appointed and given the responsibility to ensure that: -

- The necessary and identified precautions are taken

- To check and ensure Safety at each stage of the task and, may need to be present while work is going on.
- Be familiar with and understand the entry hazards
- Verify entry permits, including tests and procedures before endorsing each permit
- Cancel or suspend entry when required
- Verify rescue services are available and means of communication is operable.
- Notify employer immediately if rescue service is unavailable.
- Remove any unauthorized individuals and prevent their entry into the space
- Determine if acceptable conditions are maintained as conditions change and whenever responsibility is transferred
- Sign the entry permit to authorize entry
- Make the permit available by posting at the portal
- Terminate entry and
  - Cancel the permit when the operation is completed
  - Suspend/cancel the permit and fully reassess the space before allowing re-entry when a temporary condition that is not allowed arises in or near the space
  - Cancel the permit if a non-allowed condition arises

4. **Attendant:** The person to be posted at the entrance of the Confined space has to be able to continuously observe the person inside the Confined space (that is, to keep watch). In case of an emergency situation, he is expected to notice it and raise alarm appropriately. Also, whenever there is a Confined space entry work going on, there should be one or more persons within calling distance of the attendant at the Confined space opening to help in emergency rescue operation. The attendant should also be empowered to control the access into the Confined space by unauthorized persons (using applicable and agreed Restricted Entry Procedure).

Other functions include:

- Must be familiar with and understand the hazards

- Be aware of the possible behavioral effects of exposure

- Continuously maintain an accurate count of authorized entrants and ensure accurate means to identifying who is in the permit space at any time

- Remain outside the space until relieved by another attendant

- Communicate with entrants about their status and alert them to evacuate

- Assess activities inside and outside the space to determine if there is a need to evacuate

- Summon rescue and emergency services

- Prevent unauthorized persons from entering the space

- Perform non-entry rescues

- Perform no duties that interfere with their primary attendant duties

- At least one attendant must be outside the permit space during the duration of operations

- Attendants may be assigned to more than one permit space only if they can effectively perform their duties at each space

- They can be at any location outside the space as long as they can effectively perform their duties

- If they are attending more than one space, the means to do so and procedures for responding to emergencies must be included in the permit.

5. **Entrant**: Is the person authorized to enter the confined space. The Roles of an entrant include:

   - Must be familiar with and understand the hazards (including mode, signs and symptoms, consequences)

   - Properly use required equipment

   - Communicate with the attendant about entrant status

   - Alert attendant of the need to evacuate the space

   - Exit the space as quickly as possible when so ordered or if a dangerous situation is detected

CHAPTER SEVEN

HOT WORK IN A CONFINED SPACE

Hot Work is done where a flame is used or a source of ignition may be produced such as, flame-cutting, welding, grinding, etc.

All internal-combustion engines such as welding machines, should be kept outside the Confined Space and away from the Access/Egress and other openings of the Confined space. This is to eliminate the possibility of generating hazardous gases such as Carbon-monoxide when the hot work activities are ongoing in the Confined Space.

Hot work should not normally be performed inside a Confined space unless: -

- All flammable gases, liquids and vapors are removed prior to the start of any Hot work
- Mechanical ventilation (where applicable) is used to: -
    - ❖ Keep the concentration of any explosive or flammable hazardous substance less than 10% of its Lower Explosive Limit (LEL) and;
    - ❖ Make sure that the oxygen content in the Confined space is not enriched. Oxygen content within the Confined space should be less than 23% but greater than 19.5% so as to support life without presenting fire/explosion hazards.

It is also worthy to note that: -

- Confined space can easily be formed
- Inert gases (e.g. Nitrogen) used in purging Confined spaces of flammable/explosive/hazardous gases or vapors, in quite small amounts, can reduce the oxygen content to dangerous levels in the Confined space
- Whatsoever is introduced into a Process Plant must always exit out of the Plant in any form such as intermediates and finished products. Their chemical and physical characteristics and, mode of exits should also be considered.

NOTE: While performing hot work, the concentrations of oxygen and combustible materials should be monitored to ensure that the oxygen levels remain within the proper safe range and, the levels for combustible materials do not get higher than 10% of the LEL. In special cases, this may not be possible; hence, additional precautions have to be taken prior to entering into the Confined space to ensure the safety of the workers.

These special precautions include: -

- If potential flammable atmospheric hazards are identified during the initial testing, the Confined space should be cleansed or purged and ventilated, and re-tested before entry into the Confined space is allowed. Only after the outcome of the atmospheric air testing is within allowable limits (e.g. oxygen concentration being 19.5% - 23%)

should the Confined space entry be allowed as gas used for purging can be extremely hazardous.

- All potentially hazardous energy sources must be de-energized and, locked out and tagged out prior to entry into the Confined space so that equipment cannot be turned on accidentally.
- Ensure that: -
    a) Any liquids or free-flowing solids are removed from the Confined space to eliminate the risk of drowning or suffocation
    b) All pipes should be physically disconnected or isolation flanges bolted in place, tagged and documented as applicable. Closing valve(s) is not sufficient as there may be leakages
    c) A barrier is present to prevent liquids or free-flowing solids from entering the Confined space
    d) The opening for entry into and exit from the Confined space is large enough to allow the passage of a person using personal protective equipment (PPE)

The next Chapter will highlight some statutory requirements for Confined space entry.

CHAPTER EIGHT

STATUTORY REQUIREMENTS FOR SAFE ENTRY INTO CONFINED SPACE

Many people have been killed (in accidents occurring) inside Tanks and other Confined spaces.

Sometimes they have entered without permission to do so or, merely put their head inside an open man-way to inspect the inside;

Sometimes entry was authorized but not all of the hazardous material(s) had been removed or, it had leaked back in because isolation was poor;

Sometimes the hazardous material was deliberately introduced in order to carry out tests;

Sometimes potentially hazardous power devices were not properly de-energized, locked out and tagged out;

Sometimes people have entered a Confined space to rescue someone who has collapsed inside and had been overcome themselves.

The effects of all these will lead to high accident costs on the Organization thereby leading to serious financial implications on the Organization's revenues. Therefore, the importance of Accident prevention can never be over-emphasized.

To forestall accidents in Confined space entry activities (as in other applicable cases), compliance with relevant provisions of applicable Legislations and Regulations is of utmost importance.

These provisions are the expected acceptable minimum requirement for safety. Individual Organizations can then set up their own minimum Safety Standards which should not be lower than the level of standards set by the Legislation but, can be above it.

In individual Countries like Nigeria, these Legislative provisions are outlined in the FACTORIES' ACT (1990) which is in accordance with the International Labor Organization's requirement.

Also depending on the type of activities carried out by the Companies, there are other complimentary Legislations which include, but not limited to: -

Mineral Oils (Safety) Regulations (L.N. 45 of 1963) and 1997

The summary of their provisions are that Companies are to provide the following, among others, for their employees: -
- A safe place of work
- A safe means of work
- A safe system of work

It also highlights punitive measures that can be used against defaulters

Specifically, with regards to Confined space entry activities, sections 29 and 30 of the Nigeria's Factories' Act of 1987 stipulate precautions in places where dangerous fumes are likely to be present; and precautions with respect to explosives or other inflammable dust, gas, vapor or substance.

Other relevant Legislations/Regulations with regards to Confined space entry activities include: -

- The Confined spaces Regulations (1997)
- The Management of Health and Safety at Work Regulations (1999)
- The control of Substances Hazardous to Health Regulations (2002 as amended)
- The Personal Protection Equipment at Work Regulations (1992 as amended)
- The provision and Use of Work Equipment Regulations (1998)
- Electricity at Work Regulations (1989)
- Work Place (Health, Safety and Welfare) Regulations (1992)

Their provisions concerning certain aspects of safe works in Confined spaces may be summarized as follows: -

"No one may enter or remain for any purpose in a Confined space which has at any time contained or is likely to contain fumes liable to cause a person to be overcome, unless;

1. He is wearing approved breathing apparatus
2. He has been authorized to enter by a Responsible person
3. Where practicable, he is wearing a belt with a rope securely attached

4. A person keeping watch outside and capable of pulling him out is holding the free end of the rope

Alternatively, a person may enter or work in a Confined space without Breathing Apparatus provided that: -

1. Effective steps have been taken to avoid ingress of dangerous fumes
2. Sludge or other deposits liable to give off dangerous fumes have been removed
3. The space contains no other material liable to give off such fumes
4. The space has been adequately ventilated and tested for fumes
5. There is a supply of air adequate for respiration
6. The space has been certified by a Responsible person as being safe for entry for a specified period without Breathing Apparatus.

The person who enters the Confined space must be warned when the safe period specified in (6) above will expire.

In all cases, a sufficient supply of approved Breathing Apparatus, belts and ropes, and oxygen must be kept readily available, properly maintained and regularly examined.

Oxygen deficient Atmospheres: No one may enter or remain in Confined space in which the Atmosphere is liable to be deficient in oxygen unless either he is wearing approved Breathing Apparatus, or the space has been and remains adequately ventilated and a responsible person has tested and certified it as safe for entry without Breathing Apparatus" (HSE 1980).

Access and egress: According to HSE (1980), The Factories Act (1961),Section 30 specifies that unless there are other adequate means of access/egress, "Confined spaces should be provided with man-hole entrances which may be Rectangular, Oval, or Circular in shape and, not less than 18inches by 16inches (458mm x 407mm) or, if Circular, 18inches (458mm) in diameter.

In the case of Tank-wagons and other mobile Plants, the minimum dimensions are 16inches by 14inches (407mm x 356mm) or, if Circular, 16inches (407mm) in diameter."

In the case of small vessels, it may not be possible to achieve the provision of the minimum standard access/egress, e.g., small pressure vessel of less than 500g gallons (2000L) capacity. "Such vessels should be constructed in such a way that it will be possible to remove the top completely for cleaning, maintenance or, alternately, arrangements should be made for this work to be done without entering the vessel, for example, by installation of "in-situ" cleaning equipment."

Other highlights of the Statutory provisions include: -
- Provision of appropriate Trainings for the workers
- Provision for appropriate maintenance of equipment and tools
- Provision for the preparation of safe work procedures
- Provision for adequate provision of Personal Protective Equipment (PPE) for the workers.

Reference can also be made to IOGP report 577 – Fabrication site construction safety Practices, version 1, published February 2017 for Confined space entry

REFERENCES

HSE (1980): Entry into Confined spaces, Guidance Note, General series 5; Health and Safety Executive, Wales (1980). IOGP report 577 – Fabrication site construction safety Practices, version 1, published February 2017

NIGERIA FACTORIES ACT (No. 16 of 1987); NATLEX-National Laws on Labour, Social Security and related Human Rights, 1987.

Workplace Safety and Health Council (2010): Technical Advisory on Working Safely in Confined Spaces; **Published in January 2010 by the Workplace Safety and Health Council in collaboration with the Ministry of Manpower.**

BAMBER, L (1980), "INCIDENT RECALL"
       "a lack of Progress Report".
       Health and Safety at work 2, New York.

KLETZ, T. A (2003). "Still Going Wrong!: Case histories of Process Plant disasters and how they could have been avoided" Butterworth-Heinemann, 200 Wheeler Road, Burlington, MA 01803 P.xv.

OMOKIRI, R (2006). "Essential Duties of a Safety Officer"
       Mafinew and Sons Nigeria Ltd, Port Harcourt, Nigeria.

Confined spaces: A brief guide to working safely INDG258
       (HSE UK)